CW00796853

ANATOMICAL PLATES

OF THE

BONES AND MUSCLES,

DIMINISHED FROM

ALBINUS,

FOR

THE USE

OF

Students in Anatomy, and Artists:

ACCOMPANIED BY

Explanatory Maps.

BY

ROBERT HOOPER, M. D.

Licentiate of Physic of the University of Oxford, and of the Royal College
of Physicians of London; Physician to the St. Mary-le-bone
Infirmary, &c.

THIRD EDITION.

LONDON:

PRINTED FOR J. MURRAY, FLEET STREET; AND
CONSTABLE AND CO. EDINBURGH.

1807.

S. Gosnell, Printer, Little Queen Street, Holborn.

PREFACE.

The Anatomical Plates here presented to the Public were designed to accompany the last edition of the ANATOMIST's VADE-MECUM; but the great and unexpected demand for that work obliged the Author to put it to press before the plates could be executed. They now form a separate Fasciculus, and may either be attached to that work, or not.

It is hoped, that the Explanatory Maps which accompany the plates, will enable the student, for whose use they principally are intended, to obtain, with greater facility, an accurate knowledge of the situation of the bones and muscles. Should the plan be approved, this fasciculus will be followed by others, to illustrate the situation, form, &c. of the viscera, blood-vessels, nerves, absorbents, &c.

The reader will be pleased to observe, that, in order to preserve the beauty of the engravings, no references are inserted; and that, with respect to those of the maps, the same numbers are mostly affixed to the same part, in whatever plate they may occur (thus, for example, 185, which occurs in several plates, is always put to mark the Gastrocnemius externus: thus, 86 will be found affixed to the different plates in which the Psoas magnus is exhibited, &c. &c.); and to obviate the tediousness which attends turning over leaves to consult one general reference, the references of each plate are printed on the opposite side.

(4)

This plate exhibits a front view of the skeleton.

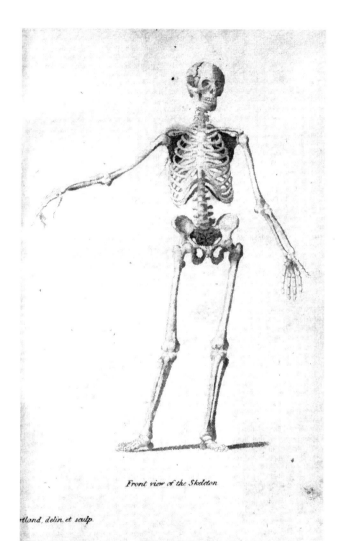

Front view of the Skeleton.

rtland, delin. et sculp.

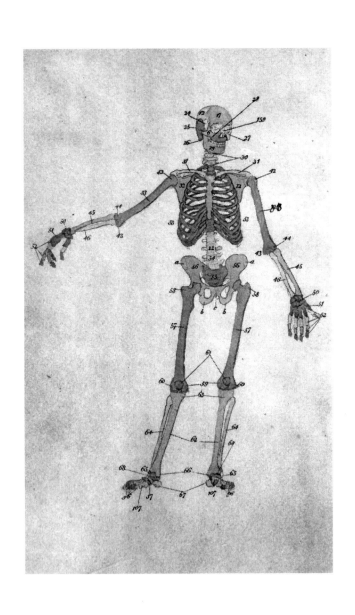

A Map of the Skeleton anteriorly.

REFERENCES.

12. Os parietale.
17. — frontis.
24. — sphænoideum.
25. — temporis.
26. Mastoid process.
27. Os malæ.
28. — maxillare superius.
29. — maxillare inferius.
30. Cervical vertebræ.
31. Clavicle.
32. Scapula.
33. Humerus.
37. Small bones of the tarsus.
42. Head of the humerus.
43. Internal condyle of the humerus.
44. External condyle of the humerus.
45. Radius.
46. Ulna.
50. Eight bones of the carpus.
51. Metacarpal bones.
52. Phalanges of the fingers.
53. Ribs.
54. Lumbar vertebræ.
55. Sacrum.
56. Os innominatum: — *a*, ilium; *b*, ischium; *c*, pubis.
57. Femur.
58. The great trochanter.
59. Internal condyle of the femur.
60. External condyle of the femur.
61. Patella.
62. Tibia.
63. Head of the tibia.
64. Fibula.
65. External ankle.
66. Internal ankle.
67. Os calcis.
68. Astragalus.
96. Phalanges of the toes.
107. Metatarsal bones.
159. Os nasi.

A back view of the skeleton.

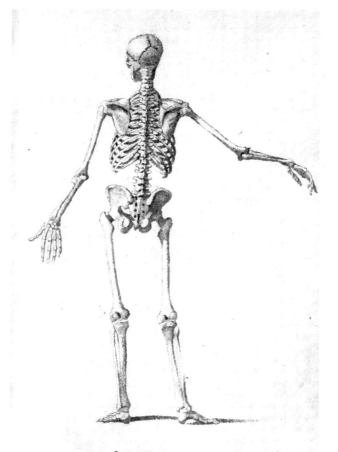

Back view of the Skeleton.

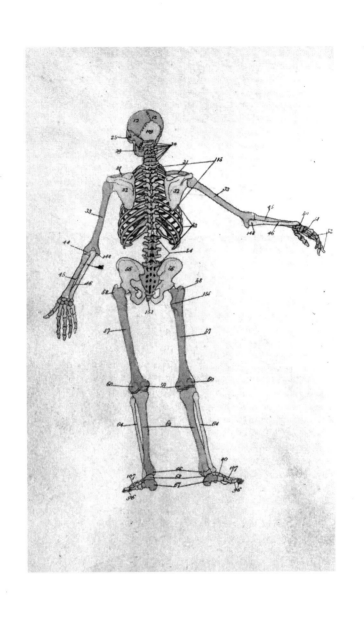

A Map of the Skeleton posteriorly.

12. Os parietale.
25. — temporis.
29. Lower jaw.
30. Cervical vertebræ.
31. Clavicle.
32. Scapula.
33. Humerus.
45. Radius.
46. Ulna.
50. Eight carpal bones.
51. Metacarpal bones.
52. Phalanges of the fingers.
53. Ribs.
54. Lumbar vertebræ.
56. Os innominatum.
57. Femur.
58. Great trochanter.

59. Internal condyle of the femur.
60. External condyle of the femur.
62. Tibia.
64. Fibula.
66. Internal ankle.
67. Os calcis.
68. Astragalus.
80. Tarsal bones.
96. Phalanges of the toes.
107. Metatarsal bones.
109. Os occipitis.
115. Dorsal vertebræ.
148. Olecranon.
153. Os coccygis.
155. Little trochanter.

A side view of the skeleton.

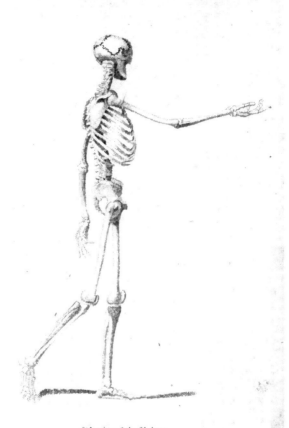

Side view of the Skeleton

md delin. et sculp.

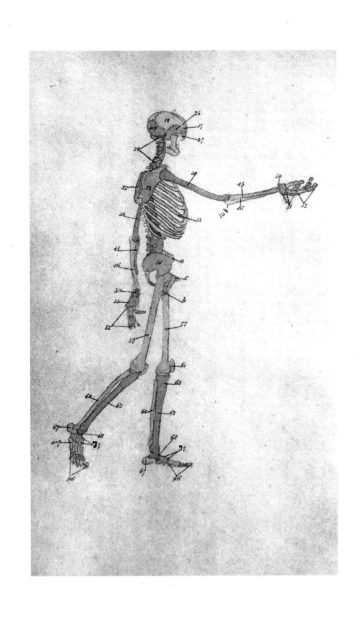

A Map of the Side View of the Skeleton.

REFERENCES.

12. Os parietale.
17. — frontis.
25. — temporis.
27. — malæ.
30. Cervical vertebræ.
32. Scapula.
38. Os humeri.
45. Radius.
46. Ulna.
50. Carpal bones.
51. Metacarpal bones.
52. Phalanges of the fingers.
53. Ribs.

56. Os innominatum : — a, iliac portion ; b, ischium; c, pubis.
57. Os femoris.
57. Bones of the tarsus.
61. Patella.
62. Tibia.
63. Head of the tibia.
64. Fibula.
67. Os calcis.
68. Astragalus.
96. Phalanges of the toes.
107. Metatarsal bones.
109. Os occipitale.
148 Olecranon

This plate represents the outermost order of muscles, as they appear when the body is deprived of its common integuments and fasciæ.

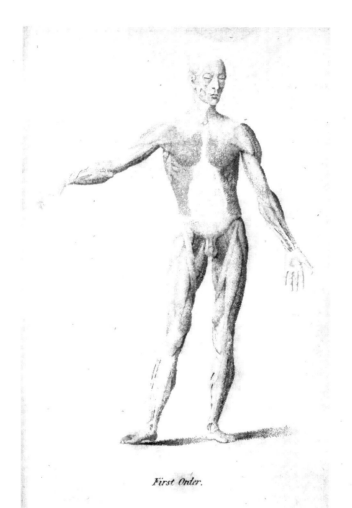

First Order.

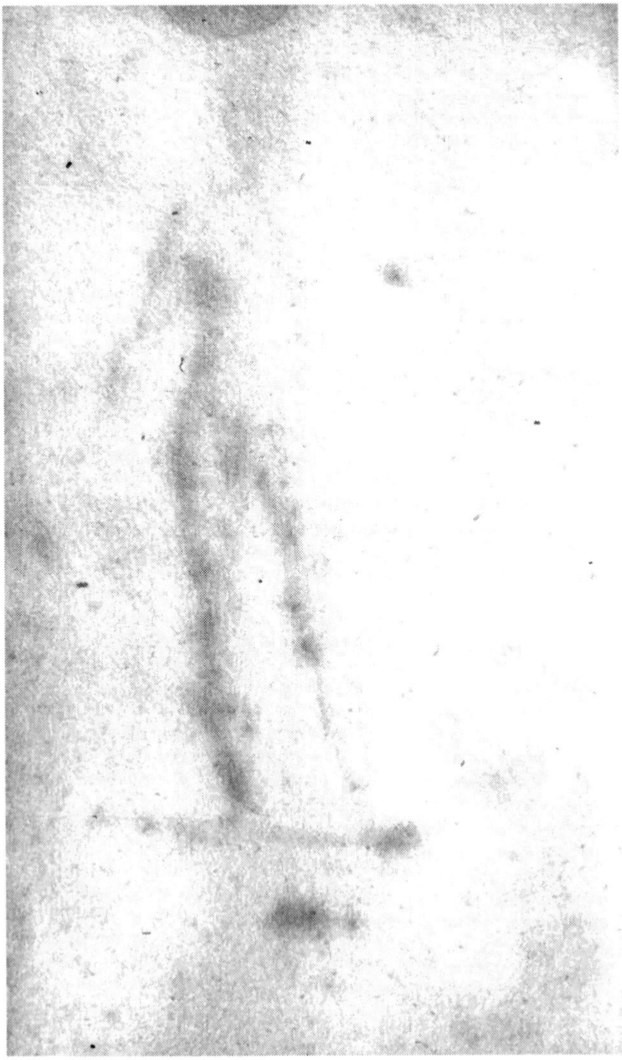

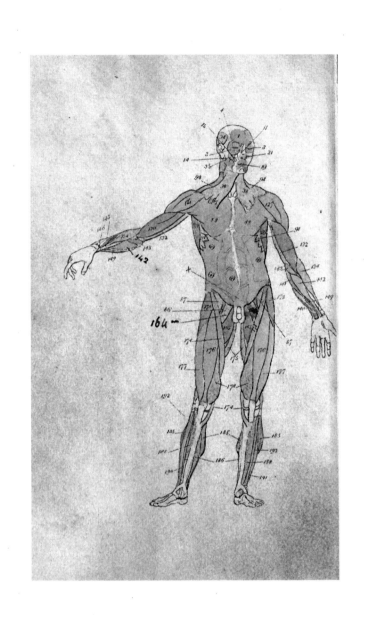

A Map of the First Order of Muscles.

REFERENCES.

1. Occipito-frontalis.
3. Orbicularis palpebrarum.
4. Levator palpebræ supe-
rioris.
11. —— labii superioris
alæque nasi.
14. Zygomaticus major.
15. —— minor.
19. Orbicularis oris.
21. Constrictor nasi.
35. Masseter.
38. Platysma myoides.
69. Obliquus externus abdominis.
86. Psoas magnus.
88. Pectoralis major.
91. Serratus major anticus.
98. Trapezius.
99. Latissimus dorsi.
127. Deltoides.
130. Biceps flexor cubiti.
87 Iliacus internus

132. Triceps extensor cubiti.
134. Supinator radii longus.
140. Flexor carpi ulnaris.
141. Palmaris longus.
142. Flexor carpi radialis.
143. Pronator radii teres.
145. Extensor ossis metacarpi
pollicis manus.
146. —— primi interno-
dii.
149. Flexor digitorum sublimis. *164 Pectoralis*
165. Triceps adductor femoris.
173. Tensor vaginæ femoris.
174. Sartorius.
177. Vastus externus.
178. —— internus.
185. Gastrocnemius externus.
186. —————— internus.
* Abdominal rings.

176 Rectus Femoris
190 Proneus Longus
191 —— Brevis
192 Extensor longus digito
188 Tibialis anticus
175 Gracilis

Several of the outermost layer of muscles are removed in this
figure, to bring the second order into view.

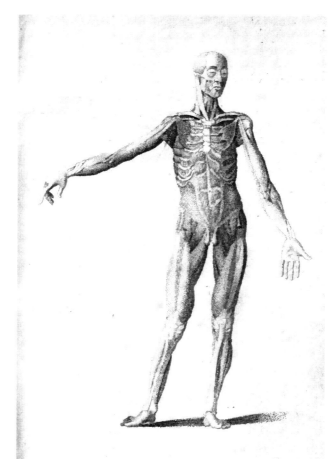

Second Order.

rtland delin. et sculp.

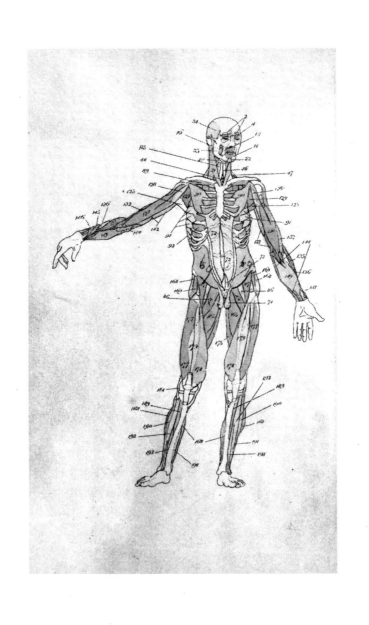

A Map of the Second Layer of Muscles.

2. Corrugator supercilii.
4. Levator palpebræ supe-rioris.
13. ———— anguli oris.
16. Buccinator.
18. Depressor anguli oris.
22. Levator menti.
34. Temporalis.
35. Masseter.
39. Sterno-cleido-mastoideus.
40. Digastricus.
46. Sterno-hyoideus.
47. Omo-hyoideus.
48. Sterno-thyroideus.
69. Obliquus internus abdo-minis.
72. Rectus abdominis.
73. Pyramidalis.
74. Cremaster.
86. Psoas magnus.
87. Iliacus internus.
89. Subclavius.
90. Pectoralis minor.
91. Serratus major anticus.
95. Rectus internus capitis major.
125. Teres minor.
128. Coraco-brachialis.
129. Subscapularis.
130. Biceps flexor cubiti.

132. Triceps extensor cubiti.
135. Extensor carpi radialis longior.
136. ———— carpi radialis brevior.
140. Flexor carpi ulnaris.
145. Extensor ossis metacarpi pollicis manus.
146. ———— primi internodii.
149. Flexor digitorum sublimis
151. ———— longus pollicis.
164. Pectinalis.
165. Triceps adductor femoris
168. Gluteus medius.
169. ———— minimus.
175. Gracilis.
177. Vastus externus.
178. ———— internus.
179 Cruræus.
186. Flexor longus pollicis pedis.
189. Tibialis posticus.
190. Peroneus longus.
191. ———— brevis.
192. Extensor longus digito-rum pedis.
193. ———— proprius polli-cis pedis.
194. Flexor longus digitorum pedis.

This plate exhibits the third layer of muscles; the first and second orders having been removed.

Third Order.

[...]land delin et sculp.

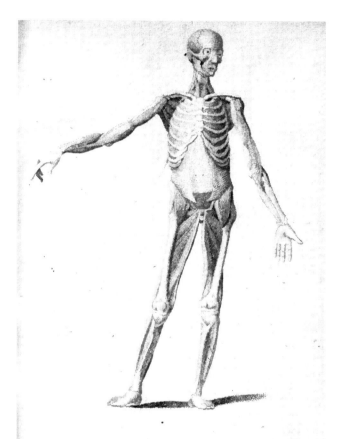

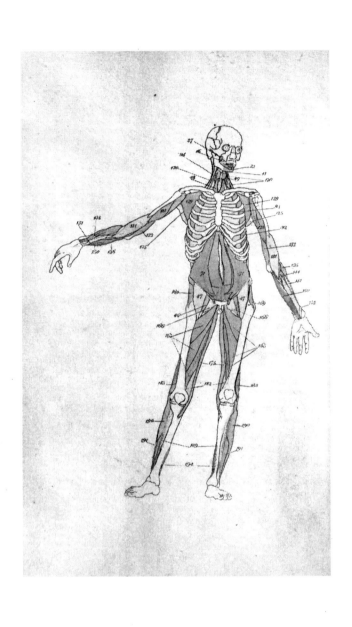

A Map of the Third Order of Muscles.

REFERENCES.

16. Buccinator.
22. Levator menti.
37. Pterygoideus externus.
41. Mylo-hyoideus.
48. Sterno-thyroideus.
49. Hyo-thyroideus.
71. Transversalis abdominis.
86. Psoas magnus.
87. Iliacus internus.
92. Intercostales externi.
93. ————— interni.
95. Rectus internus capitis major.
120. Scalenus.
125. Teres minor.
128. Coraco-brachialis.
129. Subscapularis.
131. Brachialis internus.
132. Triceps extensor cubiti.

135. Extensor carpi radialis longior.
136. ————— radialis brevior.
144. Supinator radii brevis.
150. Flexor digitorum profundus.
151. ———— longus pollicis.
152. Pronator radii quadratus.
165. Triceps adductor femoris.
166. Obturator externus.
169. Gluteus minimus.
175. Gracilis.
182. Semimembranosus.
183. Biceps flexor cruris.
189. Tibialis posticus.
190. Peroneus longus.
191. ———— brevis.
194. Flexor longus digitorum pedis.

The three outermost orders of muscles are removed from this
figure, to bring the fourth or last layer into view.

Fourth Order

land delin. et sculp.

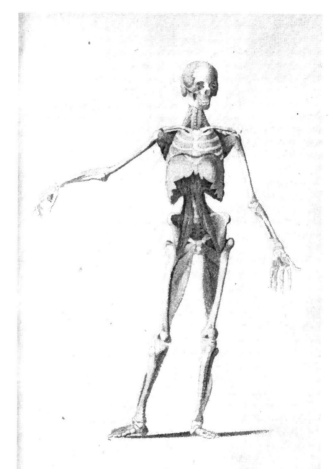

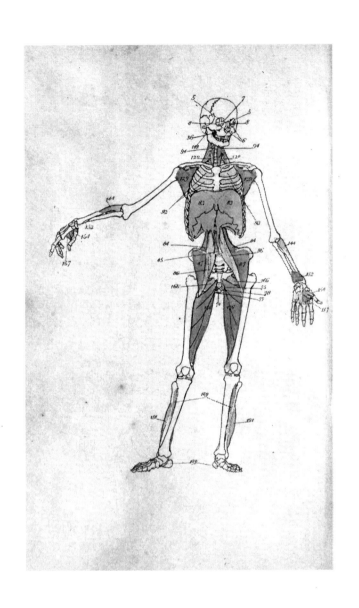

A Map of the last Layer of Muscles anteriorly.

REFERENCES.

5. Rectus superior oculi.
6. ———- inferior oculi.
7. ——— internus oculi.
8. ——— externus oculi.
36. Pterygoideus internus.
75. Erector penis.
76. Accelerator urinæ.
77. Transversalis perinæi.
78. Sphincter ani.
84. Quadratus lumborum.
85. Psoas parvus.
86. ——— magnus.
87. Iliacus internus.
91. Intercostales externi.

93. Intercostales interni.
94. Longus colli.
118. Obliquus capitis superior.
120. Scalenus.
129. Subscapularis.
144. Supinator radii brevis.
152. Pronator radii quadratus.
154. Flexor brevis pollicis manus.
157. Adductor pollicis manus.
166. Obturator externus.
176. Triceps adductor femoris.
189. Tibialis posticus.
191. Peroneus brevis.

(18)

This plate exhibits the outermost layer of muscles posteriorly, as they appear when the common integuments and fasciæ are removed.

First order.

nd delin. et sculp.

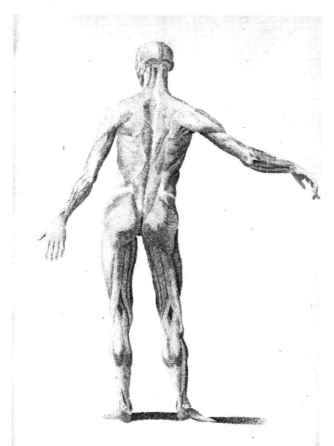

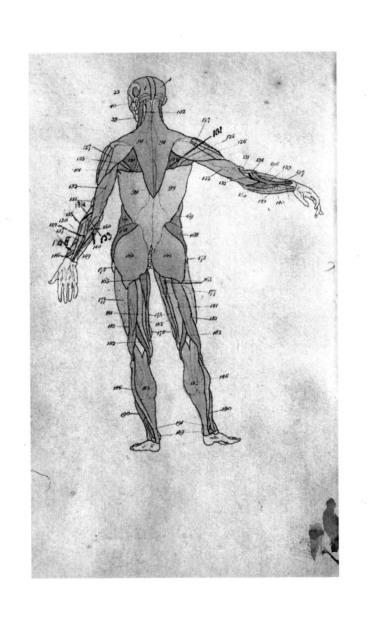

*A Map of the outermost Layer of Muscles on the posterior
Surface of the Body.*

REFERENCES.

1, Occipito-frontalis.
23. Superior auris.
39. Sterno-cleido-mastoideus.
40. Digastricus.
69. Obliquus externus abdominis.
98. Trapezius.
99. Latissimus dorsi.
101. Rhomboideus.
102. Splenius.
124. Infra-spinatus.
125. Teres minor.
126. —— major.
127. Deltoides.
131. Brachialis internus.
132. Triceps extensor cubiti.
133. Anconeus.
134. Supinator radii longus.
135. Extensor carpi radialis longior.
136. Extensor carpi radialis brevior.
137. Extensor digitorum communis.
139. —— carpi ulnaris.
140. Flexor carpi ulnaris.
145. Extensor ossis metacarpi pollicis manus.
146. —— primi internodii
149. Flexor digitorum sublimis
150. —— profundus
165. —— *Triceps adductor femoris*
168. Gluteus medius.
169. —— maximus.
173. Tensor vaginæ femoris.
175. Gracilis.
177. Vastus externus.
178. —— internus.
181. Semitendinosus.
182. Semimembranosus.
183. Biceps flexor cruris.
185. Gastrocnemius externus.
186. —— internus.
190. Peroneus longus.
191. —— *brevis*

B 2

Some of the outermost layer of muscles are removed, in this
figure, from the posterior surface of the body, to bring the
second order into view.

Second order.

irtland delin. et sculp.

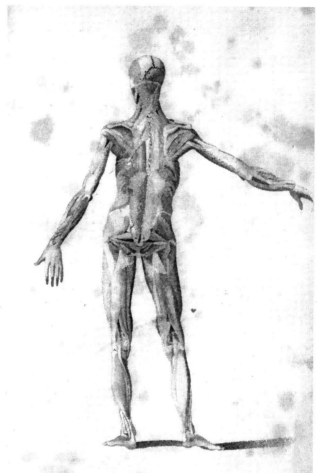

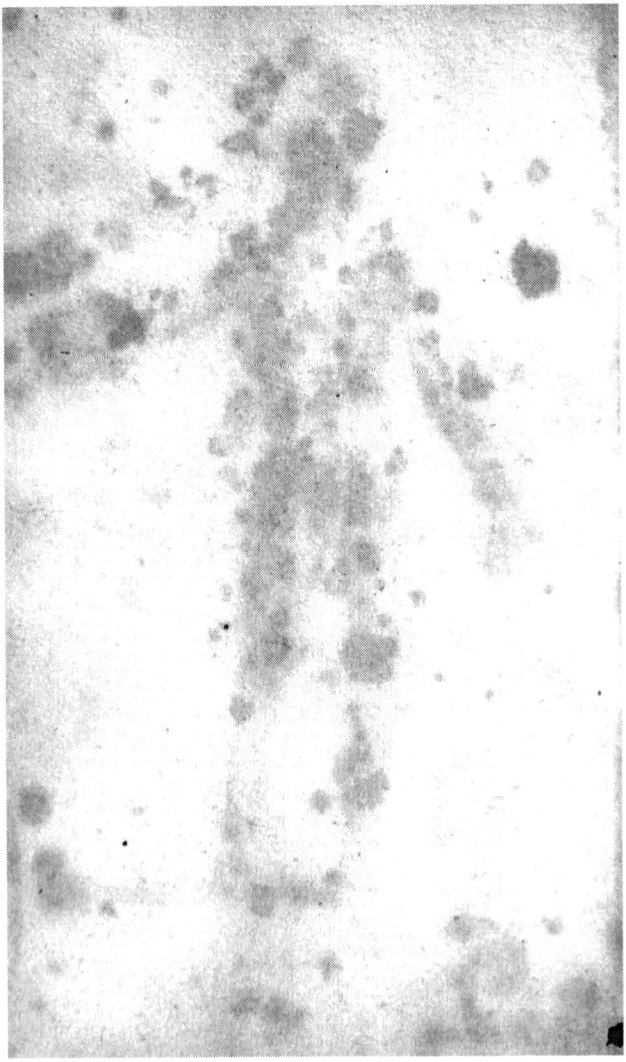

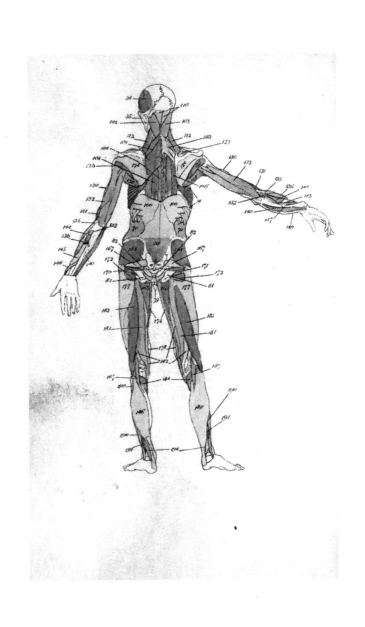

A Map of the Second Order of Muscles on the posterior Surface of the Body.

REFERENCES.

34. Temporalis.
35. Masseter.
70. Obliquus internus abdominis.
79. Levator ani.
81. Obturator internus.
82. Coccygeus.
91. Serratus major anticus.
99. Latissimus dorsi.
100. Serratus posticus inferior.
101. Rhomboideus.
102. Splenius.
103. Serratus superior posticus.
104. Spinalis dorsi.
105. Sacro-lumbalis.
108. Longissimus dorsi.
110. Complexus.
112. Levator scapulæ.
123. Supra-spinatus.
124. Infra-spinatus.
125. Teres minor.
126. —— major.
130. Biceps flexor cubiti.
131. Brachialis internus.
132. Triceps extensor cubiti.
133. Anconeus.
135. Extensor carpi radialis longior.
136. Extensor carpi radialis brevior.

140. Flexor carpi ulnaris.
144. Supinator radii brevis.
145. Extensor ossis metacarpi pollicis manus.
146. ———— primi internodii.
147. ———— secundi internodii.
149. Flexor digitorum sublimis.
165. Tricepsadductorfemoris.
167. Pyriformis.
168. Gluteus medius.
170.
171. } Gemini.
172. Quadratus femoris.
175. Gracilis.
177. Vastus externus.
178. —— internus.
181. Semitendinosus.
182. Semimembranosus.
183. Biceps flexor cruris.
184. Popliteus.
186. Gastrocnemius internus.
187. Plantaris.
190. Peroneus longus.
191. ———— brevis.
194. Flexor longus digitorum pedis.

The outermost and second layer of muscles are here removed,
to exhibit the third order.

Third order.

[l]and delin. et sculp.

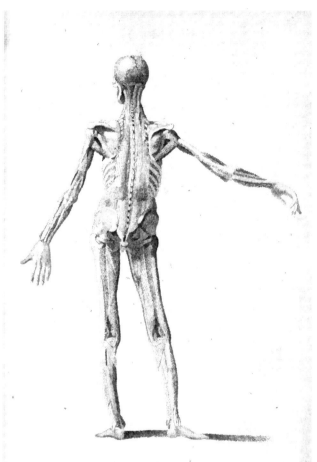

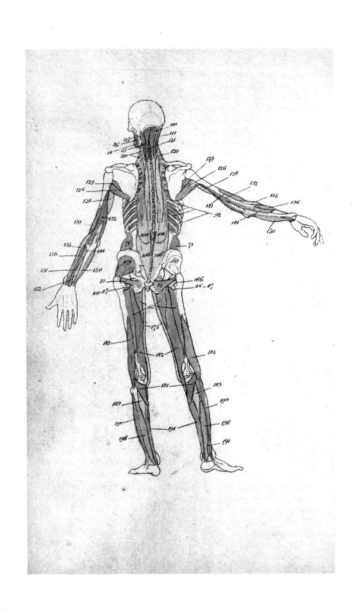

A Map of the Third Order of Muscles on the posterior
Surface of the Body.

REFERENCES.

14. Mylo-hyoideus.
16. Buccinator.
36. Pterygoideus internus.
41. Complexus.
71. Transversalis abdominis.
81. Obturator internus.
86. Psoas magnus.
87. ——— parvus.
92. Intercostales externi.
106. Sacro-lumbalis.
108. Longissimus dorsi.
110. Complexus.
111. Trachelo-mastoideus.
120. Scalenus.
121. Interspinales.
126. Teres major.
128. Coraco-brachialis.
129. Subscapularis.
131. Brachialis internus.
132. Triceps extensor cubiti.
135. Extensor carpi radialis
longior.

136. Extensor carpi radialis
brevior.
144. Supinator radii brevis.
150. Flexor digitorum sublimis.
151. ——— longus pollicis
152. Pronator radii quadratus.
165. Triceps adductor femoris.
166. Obturator externus.
169. Gluteus minimus.
175. Gracilis.
182. Semimembranosus.
183. Biceps flexor cruris.
184. Popliteus.
189. Tibialis posticus.
190. Peroneus longus.
191. ——— brevis.
194. Flexor longus digitorum
pedis.
196. ——————— pollicis
pedis.

This plate exhibits the last layer of muscles posteriorly.

Fourth order.

[…]and delin et sculp.

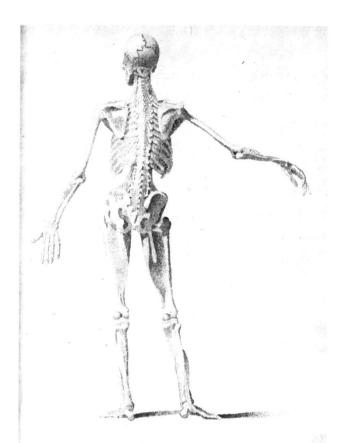

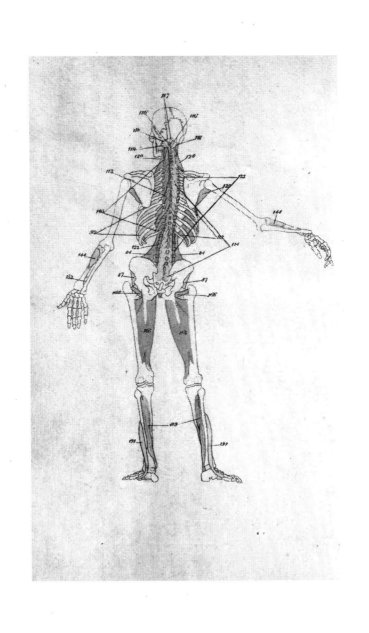

A Map of the last Order of Muscles on the posterior
Surface of the Body.

REFERENCES.

84. Quadratus lumborum.
87. Iliacus internus.
92. Intercostales externi.
93. ————— interni.
105. Levatores costarum.
113. Semispinales dorsi.
114. Multifidus spinæ.
116. Rectus capitis posticus major.
117. Rectus capitis posticus minor.

118. Obliquus capitis superior.
119. ————————— inferior.
120. Scalenus.
122. Intertransversales.
129. Subscapularis.
144. Supinator radii brevis.
152. Pronator radii quadratus.
165. Triceps adductor femoris.
166. Obturator externus.
189. Tibialis posticus.
191. Peroneus brevis.

This figure represents a side view of the external layer of
muscles, as they appear when the common integuments and
fasciæ are removed.

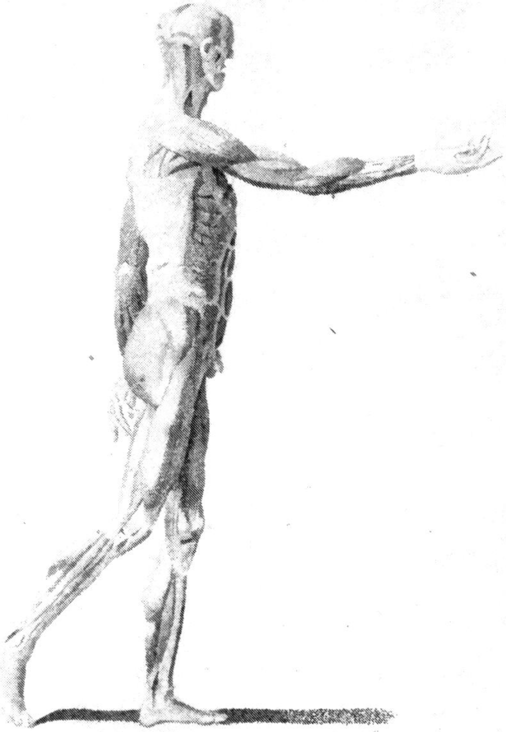

Side view of the First order.

'and delin et sculp.

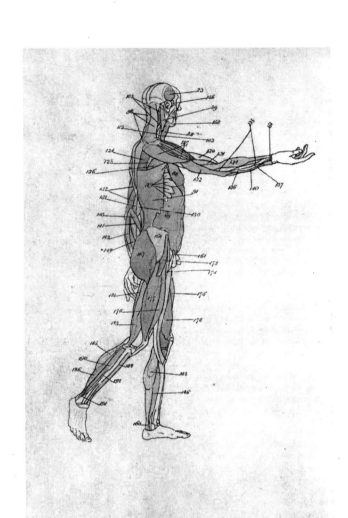

A Map of the Side View of the external Layer of Muscles.

38. Platysma myoides.
39. Sterno-cleido-mastoideus.
69. Obliquus externus abdominis.
88. Pectoralis major.
91. Latissimus dorsi.
98. Trapezius.
99. Serratus major anticus.
102. Splenius.
112. Levator scapulæ.
124. Infra-spinatus.
125. Teres minor.
126. ——— major.
127. Deltoides.
130. Biceps flexor cubiti.
131. Brachialis internus.
132. Triceps extensor cubiti.
134. Supinator radii longus.
135. Extensor carpi radialis longior.
136. Extensor carpi radialis brevior.
137. ——— digitorum communis.
140. Flexor carpi ulnaris.
141. Palmaris longus.

142. Flexor carpi ulnaris. *radia*
143. Pronator radii teres.
149. Flexor digitorum sublimis.
151. ——— longus pollicis.
156. Anterior auris.
158. Depressor anguli oris.
160. Tendo Achillis.
164. Pectinalis.
167. Gluteus maximus.
168. ——— medius.
173. Tensor vaginæ femoris.
174. Sartorius.
176. Rectus femoris.
177. Vastus externus.
178. ——— internus.
181. Semitendinosus.
183. Biceps flexor cruris.
185. Gastrocnemius externus.
186. ——————— internus.
188. Tibialis anticus.
190. Peroneus longus.
191. ——— brevis.
192. Extensor longus digitorum pedis.

LATELY PUBLISHED.

1. THE ANATOMIST's VADE-MECUM : containing the ANATOMY, PHYSIOLOGY, MORBID APPEARANCES, &c. of the HUMAN BODY; the Art of making Anatomical Preparations, &c. To which are added, Anatomical, Physiological, Medical, and Surgical Questions for Students. By ROBERT HOOPER, M. D. Licentiate in Physic of the University of Oxford, and the Royal College of Physicians in London; Physician to the St. Mary-le-bone Infirmary, &c. The SEVENTH EDITION, in one closely printed Volume, small 8vo. 9s.

2. ANATOMICAL PLATES of the THORACIC and ABDOMINAL VISCERA; accompanied by Explanatory Maps, for the Use of Students. By the same Author. 5s.

3. JOHN GOTTLIEB WALTER's PLATES of the THORACIC and ABDOMINAL NERVES, reduced from the Original, as published by Order of the Royal Academy of Sciences at Berlin: accompanied by coloured Explanations, and a Description of the Par Vagum, Great Sympathetic and Phrenic Nerves. 4to. 18s.

4. A SYSTEM of DISSECTIONS, explaining the Anatomy of the Human Body, the Manner of displaying the Parts, and their Varieties in Disease. By CHARLES BELL, Fellow of the Royal College of Surgeons, &c. SECOND EDITION, folio, 2l. 7s.

5. THE LONDON DISSECTOR: containing a Description of the Muscles, Vessels, Nerves, and Viscera, of the Human Body, as they appear on Dissection; with Directions for their Demonstration. By a Member of the Royal College of Surgeons. In one closely-printed Volume 12mo. 5s. in boards.

"This will be found a very useful guide to the student in the prosecution of his anatomical researches. It is superior to other works of a similar kind and extent, in describing not the muscles merely, but the various parts, blood-vessels, nerves, &c. as they come into view under the knife of the dissector.

A knowledge of the relative situation of parts is thus acquired; a point of the first magnitude to the practical surgeon. As the chief intention of the work is to teach the art of dissecting, the muscles are demonstrated in their order of situation, which is the only method that can be pursued in actual dissection." Medical and Chirurgical Review, 1804, vol. xi. p. 62.

6. PRACTICAL OBSERVATIONS on URINARY GRAVEL and STONE; on the Diseases of the Bladder and Prostate Gland; and on Strictures of the Urethra. By HENRY JOHN-STON, Fellow of the Royal College of Surgeons of Edinburgh. 8vo. 5s. in boards.

7. ESSAY on the PATHOLOGY of the HUMAN EYE. By JAMES WARDROP, Fellow of the Royal College of Surgeons, Edinburgh. The various morbid appearances of the Eye are illustrated by coloured Engravings by MEADOWS, MEDLAND, MADDOCKS, HEATH, &c. after Drawings by Mr. SYME. Royal 8vo.

8. ILLUSTRATIONS of some of the INJURIES to which the LOWER LIMBS are exposed, accompanied by coloured Engravings. By C. B. TRYE. 4to. 7s. 6d

9. PRACTICAL OBSERVATIONS on the NATURAL HISTORY and CURE of the VENEREAL DISEASE. By JOHN HOWARD, Member of the College of Surgeons, London. A new Edition, considerably improved, in Two Volumes 8vo. with Plates, price 18s.

10. TREATISE on GONORRHŒA VIRULENTA and LUES VENEREA. By BENJAMIN BELL, Edinburgh. SECOND EDITION, 2 vol. 8vo. 16s.

11. OUTLINES of the THEORY and PRACTICE of MIDWIFERY. By ALEXANDER HAMILTON, M.D. F.R.S. Professor of Midwifery in the University, and Fellow of the Royal College of Physicians, Edinburgh. The FIFTH EDITION, 8vo. 7s. 6d. in boards.

12. THE LONDON PRACTICE of MIDWIFERY, in plain and familiar Language, for the Use of Students. Including the Management of Women during Pregnancy, and after Delivery, with the Treatment necessary in the principal Diseases of Children. SECOND EDITION, carefully revised, and corrected throughout. In a neat Pocket Volume. 7s. boards.

13. THE MODERN PRACTICE of PHYSIC; which points
out the Characters, Causes, Symptoms, Prognostic, Morbid Appearances, and improved Method of treating the Diseases of
all Climates. By ROBERT THOMAS, M. D. The Second
Edition, in one neat and closely printed Volume, 8vo. 14s.

This Work has been carefully revised; a few Diseases, which
were omitted in the First Edition, are now inserted; and a very
large portion of new and important Matter has been added.

" This is a judicious compilation of facts, from the best wri-
ters, in which the different subjects are treated with brevity and
perspicuity. Dr. Thomas has abridged with judgment, has
added modern opinions and discoveries, has frequently intro-
duced the result of his own experience, and his performance
thus becomes an useful Compendium of the present State of
Medical Practice."—*Monthly Review, June,* p. 185.

14. OBSERVATIONS on the UTILITY and ADMINISTRA-
TION of PURGATIVE MEDICINES in several Diseases.
By JAMES HAMILTON, M. D. Fellow of the Royal College
of Physicians, and of the Royal Society of Edinburgh, and Se-
nior Physician to the Royal Infirmary of that City. Second
Edition, corrected and enlarged, 8vo. 7s. 6d.

15. A PRACTICAL SYNOPSIS of the MATERIA ALIMEN-
TARIA and MATERIA MEDICA. By RICHARD PEARSON,
M. D. Member of the Royal College of Physicians, and formerly
Physician to the General Hospital, near Birmingham. A New
Edition, comprising the latest Improvements in the London,
Edinburgh, and Dublin Pharmacopœias, complete in one Vo-
lume 8vo.

16. THESAURUS MEDICAMINUM: a new Collection of
MEDICAL PRESCRIPTIONS, distributed into Twelve Classes,
and accompanied with Pharmaceutical and Practical Remarks;
exhibiting a View of the present State of the Materia Medica
and Practice of Physic in this and other Countries. By the Author of "A Practical Synopsis of the Materia Alimentaria."
Third Edition, 8vo. 7s. 6d.

17. A TREATISE on FEBRILE DISEASES, including inter-
mitting, remitting, and continued Fevers; Inflammations,
Hemorrhages, and the Profluvia: in which an Attempt is made
to present at one View, whatever, in the present State of Medicine, it is requisite for the Physician to know, respecting the

Symptoms, Causes, and Cure of those Diseases. By A. PHI-
LIPS WILSON, M. D. F. R. S. Ed. Fellow of the Royal College of Physicians, Edinburgh. SECOND EDITION, 4 vol. 8vo.
1l. 16s.

18. AN ESSAY on the NATURE of FEVER; being an Attempt to ascertain the Principles of its Treatment. By A. PHI-
LIPS WILSON, M. D. F. R. S. Ed. Fellow of the Royal College of Physicians of Edinburgh, &c. 8vo. 5s.

19. FIRST LINES of the PRACTICE of PHYSIC. By Dr.
WILLIAM CULLEN. A NEW EDITION, with a Preface by
Dr. GREGORY of Edinburgh, 2 vol. 8vo. 14s.

20. TABLES of the MATERIA MEDICA; or, A Systematic
Arrangement of all the Articles admitted by the Colleges of
London, Edinburgh, and Dublin; exhibiting a concise View of
the most material Circumstances concerning them; together with
a Number of original and selected Formulæ; to which is sub-
joined, a Table of all the Secondary Salts employed in Medicine.
By JEREMIAH KIRBY, M. D. Member of the Royal Medical
Society of Edinburgh. Small 8vo. 4s.

21. THE EDINBURGH NEW DISPENSATORY. By AN-
DREW DUNCAN, Jun. M. D. A NEW EDITION, corrected,
enlarged, and much improved. In one large and closely-printed
Volume, 8vo. with Plates, 12s.

22. AN ACCOUNT of the DISEASES of INDIA, as they
appeared in the English Fleet, and in the Naval Hospital at
Madras, in 1782 and 1783; with Observations on Ulcers, and
the Hospital Sores of that Country; comprising also, a short
Treatise on Hospitals. To which is prefixed, a View of the
Diseases of an Expedition, and Passage of a Fleet and Arma-
ment to India in 1781. By CHARLES CURTIS, formerly
Surgeon of the Medea Frigate. 8vo. 7s.

23. AN ESSAY on the DISEASES incidental to EUROPEANS
in HOT CLIMATES, with the Method of preventing their fatal
Consequences. By JAMES LIND, M. D. F. R. S. &c. A NEW
EDITION, 8vo.

24. OBSERVATIONS on the DISEASES of SEAMEN. By
GILBERT BLANE, M. D. F. R. S. S. Lond. et Ed. &c.
THIRD EDITION, 8vo. 7s.

25. A SYSTEM of ARRANGEMENT and DISCIPLINE for the MEDICAL DEPARTMENT of ARMIES. By ROBERT JACKSON, M. D. 8vo. 12s.

26. A CONCISE and SYSTEMATIC ACCOUNT of a PAINFUL AFFECTION of the NERVES of the FACE, commonly called Tic Douloureux. By S. FOTHERGILL, M. D. 8vo. 3s.

27. OBSERVATIONS on DIARRHŒA and DYSENTERY, as these Diseases appeared in the British Army, during the Campaign in Egypt in 1801. By HENRY DEWAR, M. D. SECOND EDITION, 8vo. 4s.

28. SKETCH of the REVOLUTIONS of MEDICAL SCIENCE, and VIEWS relating to its REFORM. By P. CABANIS, Member of the National Institute, &c. &c. Translated from the French, with Notes by A. HENDERSON, M.D. 8vo. 9s.

29. ELEMENTS of GALVANISM, in THEORY and PRACTICE; with a comprehensive View of its History. Containing also, Practical Directions for constructing the Galvanic Apparatus, and plain systematic Instructions for performing all the various Experiments. 2 vol. 8vo. with a great Number of Copper-plates, 1l. 1s.

30. THE CODE of HEALTH and LONGEVITY; or, a Concise View of the Principles calculated for the Preservation of Health, and the Attainment of Long Life. By Sir JOHN SINCLAIR, Bart. 4 vol. 8vo. very closely printed. 2l. 8s.

FINIS.

S. Gosnell, Printer, Little Queen Street.

CPSIA information can be obtained at www.ICGtesting.com
Printed in the USA
BVOW04s0303120615

404189BV00017B/102/P